How to Start
& Manage a
Fish Farming
Business

A Practical Way to Start Your Own Business

by Jerre G. Lewis and Leslie D. Renn

How to Start & Manage a Fish Farming Business

Lewis & Renn Associates, Inc.
Business & Professional Publishing
10315 Harmony Drive
Interlochen, Michigan 49643
(231) 275-7287

Leslie D. Renn
President

Jerre G. Lewis
Secretary-Treasurer

ISBN # 1-57916-046-8
Library of Congress Catalog Card Number
99-094155

TABLE OF CONTENTS

Chapter 1

Introduction

Selecting the right Fish Farming business opportunity requires careful, thorough evaluations of yourself. Owning your own business is as much a part of the American dream as owning a home, and for you, this urge represents one of life's most exciting challenges. This book is for those men and women who someday may go into business for themselves and for those who are already in business for themselves but wish to strengthen their entrepreneurial and managerial skills.

Entrepreneurs come in all shapes and sizes, personalities, and lifestyles. They are usually highly motivated, hard-working individuals who receive satisfaction from taking risks. Your business should interest you, not just be an income generator. Analyze your personal style. Do you like working with people? Are you a self starter, goal oriented, persistent, a risk taker, willing to work hard and long hours?

If you have been honest in evaluating yourself, you will now select the right type of business. Before you can determine which of the multitude of businesses is right for you to start, you must evaluate the businesses you want to start by asking these questions. Is the business area growing? How does the economy affect it? Who dominates its market? Once you have considered a business that satisfies your needs and interest you must prepare a formal business plan by following the outline given in this book.

Small businesses constitute a dynamic and critical sector of the U.S. economy. Every year in the United States more than 600,000 new businesses are launched by independent men and women eager to make their own decisions, express their own ideas, and be their own bosses. But running your own business is not as easy as it may seem. There can be problems with the inventory, or getting the right goods delivered on time. Yet, managing one's own business can be a personally and financially rewarding experience for an individual strong enough to meet the test. A person with stamina, maturity, and creativity, one who is willing to make sacrifices, may find making a go of a struggling enterprise an exhilarating challenge with many compensations.

Small business owners are a dedicated group of people who work hard and whose hours on the job usually exceed the nine-to-five routine. The owner's commitment is the key to many successful small businesses; an entrepreneur is able to communicate ideas, lead, plan, be patient, and work well with people.

Managing a business requires more than the possession of technical knowledge. Because most small businesses are started by technical people, such as engineers and salesmen, their managerial acumen is often less developed than their technical skills. The need to plan for management is common to every type of and size of business, and there are certain steps that must be taken. Although some of them are very elementary — such as applying for a city business permit — the most important are often complex and difficult and require the advice of specialists: accountants, attorneys, insurance brokers, and/or bankers. For almost any business though, the first step will be to translate the entrepreneur's basic idea into a concrete plan for action.

To gauge your level of entrepreneurial spirit, the following quiz was created. Please answer each question honestly and then total the columns.

ENTREPRENEURIAL QUIZ

	YES	NO	SOMETIMES
1. I am a self-starter. Nobody has to tell me how to get going.	____	____	_____
2. I am capable of getting along with just about everybody.	____	____	_____
3. I have no trouble getting people to follow my lead.	____	____	_____
4. I like to be in charge of things and see them through.	____	____	_____
5. I always plan ahead before beginning a project. I am usually the one who gets everyone organized.	____	____	_____
6. I have a lot of stamina. I can keep going as long as necessary.	____	____	_____
7. I have no trouble making decisions and can make up my mind in a hurry.	____	____	_____
8. I say exactly what I mean. People can trust me.	____	____	_____
9. Once I make my mind up to do something, nothing can stop me.	____	____	_____
10. I am in excellent health and have a lot of energy.	____	____	_____

	YES	NO	SOMETIMES

11. I have experience or technical knowledge in the business I intend to start.   _____ _____ _____

12. I feel comfortable taking risks if it is something I really believe in.   _____ _____ _____

13. I have good communication skills.   _____ _____ _____

14. I am flexible in my dealings with people and situations.   _____ _____ _____

15. I consider myself creative and resourceful.   _____ _____ _____

16. I can analyze a situation and take steps to correct problems.   _____ _____ _____

17. I think I am capable of maintaining a good working relationship with employees.   _____ _____ _____

18. I am not a dictator. I am willing to listen to employees, customers and suppliers.   _____ _____ _____

19. I am not rigid in my policies. I am willing to adjust to meet the needs of employees, customers, and suppliers.   _____ _____ _____

20. More than anything else, I want to run my own business.   _____ _____ _____

Total of Column #1 _____

Total of Column #2 _____

Total of Column #3 _____

If the total of Column #1 is the highest, then you will probably be very successful in running your own business.

If the total of Column #2 is the highest, you may find that running a business is more than you can handle.

If the total of Column #3 is the highest, you should consider taking on a partner who is strong in your weak areas.

NOTE: This quiz was adapted from the Small Business Administration publication *Checklist for Going Into Business.*

Notes _____

Chapter 2

Planning the Business

The Dream of self-employment can be fulfilled. You don't need to finance the opening of an elaborate office or facility to start your own one-person corporation either. You can start your own Fish Farming business.

Anyone preparing to run an Fish Farming business needs to learn a great deal to assure the best possible chance for success.

GETTING STARTED

The following is a list of what you need to accomplish to insure that your Fish Farming endeavor will head in the right direction.

1. Define your educational background and work experience.

2. Survey all the basic types of Fish Farming businesses.

3. Define what products or services your Fish Farming business will be marketing.

4. Define who will be using your products/services.

5. Define why they will be purchasing your products/services.

6. List all competitors in your Fish Farming marketing area.

ZONING REGISTRATIONS

Fish Farming businesses are subject to many laws and regulations enforced by state, county, township governmental units. Most jurisdictions now have codes, a zoning board, and an appeal board which regulate businesses. Areas often are zoned residential, commercial or industrial.

You must become familiar with these regulations. If you are doing business in violation of these regulations, you could be issued a cease and desist order or fined.

Certain kinds of goods cannot be produced in the home, though these restrictions vary somewhat from state-to-state. Most states outlaw home production of fireworks, drugs, poisons, explosives, sanitary/medical products and some toys.

Many localities have registration requirements for new businesses. You will need to obtain a work certificate or license from the state.

TAX REQUIREMENTS

<u>Application for Employer Identification Number</u>, Form SS-4. This registers you with the Internal Revenue Service as a business. If you have employees, you should ask for Circular E along with your ID number. Circular E explains federal income and social security tax withholding requirements.

<u>Employer's Annual Unemployment Tax Return</u>, Form 940. This is only if you have employees. It's used to report and pay the Federal Unemployment Compensation Tax.

<u>Employee's Withholding Allowance Certificate</u>, W-4. Every employee must complete the W-4 so the proper amount of income tax can be withheld from the

employee's pay. If the employee claims more than 15 allowances or a complete withholding exemption while having a salary of more than $200 a week, a copy of the W-4 must go to the IRS.

Employer's Wage and Tax Statement, W-2. Used to report to the IRS the total taxes withheld and total compensation paid to each employee per year.

Reconciliation/Transmittal of Income and Tax Statements, W-3. Used to total all information from the W-2. Sent to the Social Security Administration.

The IRS puts on monthly workshops on understanding and using these forms. Call your local IRS office for further information.

States also have various tax form requirements including: an unemployment tax form, a certificate of registration application, a sales and use tax return, an employer's quarterly contribution and payroll report, an income tax withholding registration form, an income tax withholding form, and others. Some forms apply only to employers who have employees. Your local IRS office and state Office of Taxation can provide you with listings of forms you will need to start your business. The following table outlines Federal tax form requirements.

Every small business begins with an idea — a product to be manufactured or sold, a service to be performed.

Whatever the business or its degree of complexity, the owner needs a business plan in order to transform a vision into a working operation.

This business plan should describe in writing and in figures the proposed Fish Farming business and its products, services, or manufacturing processes. It should also include an analysis of the market, a marketing strategy, an organizational plan, and measurable financial objectives.

WHAT SHOULD A BUSINESS PLAN COVER?

It should be a thorough and objective analysis of both personal abilities and business requirements for a particular product or service. It should define strategies for such functions as marketing and production, organization and legal aspects, accounting and finance. A business plan should answer such questions as:

What do I want and what am I capable of doing?
What are the most workable ways of achieving my goals?
What can I expect in the future?

There is no single best way to begin. What follows is simply a guide and can be changed to suit individual needs.

1. Define Long-term goals.
2. State short-term.
3. Set marketing strategies to meet goals and objectives.
4. Analyze available resources.
5. Assemble financial data.
6. Review plan.

Please refer to Figure 2.1 for a complete business plan outline.

The business operator with a realistic plan has the best chance for success.

Figure 2.1

BUSINESS PLAN FOR SMALL BUSINESSES

I. Type of Business

II. Location

III. Target Market

IV. Planning Process

V. Organizational Structure

VI. Staffing Procedures

VII. Market Strategy

IX. Financial Planning

X. Budgeted Balance Sheet

XI. Budgeted Income Statement

XII. Budgeted Cash Flow Statement

XIII. Break-Even Chart

Notes _____

Chapter 3

Marketing Strategies
for an Fish Farming Business

As a potential Fish Farming business owner, it is important to learn all you can about marketing. You will need to know how to identify your market and how to market your product or service.

As a business person who looks for a profit from the sale of goods, you recognize that without people who want to buy, there is no demand for the things you want to sell. Thus, it is important that, in addition to knowing about the functions of marketing, you also study the activities that will influence the consumer. When you satisfy the specific needs and wants of the customer, then he or she may be willing to pay you a price that will include a profit for you — and to make a profit is one of the reasons you have become an Fish Farming business owner. Although there are many activities connected with marketing, most of them can be classified in these categories: buy, finance, transport, standardize, store, insure, advertise and sell.

Target Market Analysis

Before you can create a successful marketing campaign, it's necessary to determine your target market (toward whom to direct your energies). The whole concept of target marketing can seem very scary at first. On the surface, targeting appears to be limiting the scope of the pool of potential customers. Many people fear that by defining a market, they will lose business. They are concerned that they will choose the wrong market. Or that other practitioners will take just anybody and therefore some of their business.

You must keep in mind that the purpose of defining your target market is to make your life easier and increase the productivity of your promotional endeavors. Many opportunities exist in this world and it's impossible to pursue them all or be everything to everyone. You need to know where to focus your energy and money when it comes to promotion and advertising.

The two most common means of market analysis are demographics and psychographics, which describe a person in terms of objective data and personality attributes.

Demographics are statistics such as:
- age
- gender
- income level
- geographic location
- occupation
- education level

Psychographics are lifestyle factors including:
- special interest activities
- philosophical beliefs
- social factors
- cultural involvements

The more you know about your potential customers, the easier it is to develop an appropriate position statement and design an effective marketing campaign. The actual number of target markets you have depends mainly upon the size of your practice and the scope of your knowledge.

Your Target Market Profile

In order to clarify your target market(s) you need to delineate the demographic and psychographic factors and then identify the characteristics your customers have in common.

Describe your current customers and those who are most likely your future customers:

What is the age range and average age of your customers?

What is the percentage of males?

What is the percentage of females?

What is the average educational level of your customers?

Where do your customers live?

What are the occupations of your customers?

Where do your customers work?

What is the average annual income level of your customers?

Of what special interest groups are your customers members?

What is the primary reason your customers use your services?

Defining Your Target Market(s)

Write a descriptive statement for each of your target markets (refer to your "Target Market Profile"). Include a brief overview of the services you are providing to that group and a detailed analysis of the characteristics of the specific clientele.

Target Market 1:

Target Market 2:

Target Market 3:

Fish Farming Business Marketing

The foundation for creating a thriving customer base.

A. Overview

This section is about clarifying your beliefs and attitudes toward your profession and determining the image you wish to portray.

1. Describe the "character" that you want for your business. Depict the image you want to convey:

2. State your philosophy in regard to your business:

3. Describe your philosophy regarding your practice in business:

B. Customer Profile

This is a descriptive analysis of your current and potential customers — who they are, what their interests are, and where you can find them. Include each of your target markets.

1. Target Market 1:

2. Target Market 2:

3. Target Market 3:

C. Competition's Marketing Assessment

The first phase in planning your promotional campaign is appraising the competition. List each of your major competitors and describe the marketing strategies they utilize. Be certain to include where and how often they advertise.

1. Major Competitor 1:

2. Major Competitor 2:

3. Major Competitor 3:

4. Major Competitor 4:

5. Major Competitor 5:

6. Major Competitor 6:

Fish Farming Marketing Planning

Outline for Marketing:

I. Produce/Service Concept
   A. Name of produce or service
   B. Descriptive characteristics of product or service
   C. Unit sales
   D. Analysis of market trends

II. Number of Customers in Market Area:
   A. Profile of customers
   B. Average customer expenditure
   C. Total market

III. Your Market Potential:
   A. Total market divided by competition
   B. Total market multiplied by percent who will buy your product

IV. Needs of Customers:
   A. Identification
   B. Pleasure
   C. Social approval
   D. Personal interest
   E. Price

V. Direct Marketing Sources:
   A. Trade magazines
   B. Trade associates
   C. Small Business Administration (SBA)
   D. Government publications
   E. Yellow Pages
   F. Marketing directories

VI. Customer Profile:
   A. Geographical
   B. Gender
   C. Age range
   D. Income brackets
   E. Occupation
   F. Educational level

Chapter 4

Promoting the Fish Farming Business

When a new business is opened, the owner must be prepared to publicize the business or its chance for success will be slim. Only a few businesses — such as those with a prime location, nationally known name, or a built-in clientele — can succeed without advertising to promote market awareness and stimulate sales.

The first purpose — promoting customer awareness — applies as much to established businesses as to newcomers.

In the Fish Farming business, you will find it easier to retain old customers than to win new ones. When old customers move away from your area, or when their buying needs change, you need new customers to maintain your sales volume. If you expect your business to gain, you will need additional new customers. New customers are those who move into your area or who have grown into your line of products because now they can afford them or they need them. We see advertising and we hear advertising all around us, and yet that is only a part of it. Through advertising, you call the attention of customers to your products.

As a small business owner, you may advertise your business through your location. People pass by and are attracted to your operation because of what you are selling. To get a better idea of what advertising is, consider some of the following functions of advertising:

1. *To inform:* Letting customers know what you have for sale through brochures, leaflets, newspapers, radio, TV, and etc.

2. *Persuade:* Persuasion is the art of leading individuals to do what you want them to do. There are sales personnel who have persuasive sales presentations, but persuasion in advertising is nonpersonal. The appeal is made through the printed or spoken words or a picture. The influence of an ad on readers occurs as purchasers choose what they want among different products, and different wants. To gain the actions you want — a sale — you must persuade a customer to examine personally what you have for sale.

3. *Reminder:* Advertising performs it's third function when it reminds those who have been persuaded to buy once that the same product will bring satisfaction. The ad will also remind a customer of the characteristics of a product purchased some time ago, and where he or she bought it. Because customers change their loyalty to a place of business, their taste for products, and often their trading area patronage, advertising is necessary to draw new customers and to hold old customers. To generate results from advertising that will be profitable to your business, you will have to produce answers to the what, where and how of advertising.

What to Advertise

The nature of your business will partially answer the question "Shall I advertise goods or services?" What are the outstanding features of your business? Is it unique in any way? Does it have strong points? Do you have something to offer that the competition is not able to duplicate? Answers to these questions will give you a start in deciding what to advertise.

Where to Advertise

Of course, you will want to advertise within your marketing area, however there are a few guidelines to remember:

A. Who are your customers?

B. What is their income range?

C. Why do they buy?

D. How do they buy? Do they pay Cash? Charge?

E. What is the radius of your market area?

How to Advertise:

In determining how to advertise, you will have to consider your dollar allocation for advertising and the media suitable to your particular kind of business. However, it is important to have a balance between the presentation of the product or service being advertised and the application of three basic principles.

1. Gain the attention of the audience.

2. Establish a need.

3. Tell where that need may be filled.

See Figure A for an outline of the different advertising media and Figure B for budget on media goals.

Figure A

Advertising Media

Media	Market Coverage	Type of Audience
Daily Newspaper	Single community or entire metro area; zoned editions sometimes available	General
Weekly Newspaper	Single community	Residents
Telephone Directory	Geographical area or occupational field served by the directory	Active shoppers for goods or services
Direct mail audience	Controlled by the advertiser	Controlled
Radio audience	Definable market area	Selected
Television audience	Definable market area	Various
Outdoor	Entire metro area	General auto drivers
Magazine	Entire metro area or magazine region	Selected audience

Promotion and Advertising Plan — Fish Farming Business

In designing your promotional plan, it's wise to use a variety of media. You must have specific goals, time lines and budgets for each marketing application

Media	Goal	Timeline	Budget

Notes _____

Chapter 5

Financial Planning for an Fish Farming Business

Financial planning is the process of analyzing and monitoring the financial performance of your business so you can assess your current position and anticipate future problem areas. The daily, monthly, seasonal, and yearly operation of your business requires attention to the figures that tell you about the firm's financial health.

Maintaining good financial records is a necessary part of doing business.

The increasing number of governmental regulations alone makes it virtually impossible to avoid keeping detailed records. Just as important is to keep them for yourself. The success of your business depends on them. An efficient system of record keeping can help you to:

- make management decisions
- compete in the marketplace
- monitor performance
- keep track of expenses
- eliminate unprofitable merchandise
- protect your assets
- prepare your financial statements

Financial skills should include understanding of the balance sheet, the profit-and-loss statement, cash flow projection, break-even analysis, and source and application of funds. In many businesses, the husband and wife run the business; it is especially important that both of them understand financial management. Most small business owners are not accountants, but they must understand the tool of financial management if they are going to be able to measure the return on their investment. Although good records are essential to good financial planning, they alone are not enough because their full use requires interpretation and analysis. The owner/manager's financial decisions concerning return on invested funds, approaches to banks, securing greater supplier credit, raising additional equity capital and so forth, can be more successful if he takes the time to develop understanding and use of the balance sheet and profit-and-loss statement.

Balance Sheet:

The balance sheet, Figure I, shows the financial condition of a business at the end of business on a specific day. It is called a balance sheet because the total assets balance with, or are equal to, total liabilities plus owner's capital balance. Current assets are those that the owner does not anticipate holding for long. This category includes cash, finished goods in inventory, and accounts receivable. Fixed assets are long-term assets, including plant and equipment. A third possible category is the intangible asset of goodwill. Liabilities are debts owed by the business, including both accounts payable, which are usually short-term, and notes payable, which are usually long-term debts such as mortgage payments. The difference between the value of the assets and the value of the liabilities is the capital. This category includes funds invested by the owner plus accumulated profits, less withdrawals.

The Income Statement:

This statement, Figure II, is also known as a profit-and loss (P&L) statement. It shows how a business has performed over a certain period of time. An income statement specifies sales, costs of sales, gross profit, expenses and net income or loss from operations.

Figure I

Financial Forecast

Opening Balance Sheet - Date

ASSETS

Current Assets

Cash and bank accounts		$
Accounts receivable		$
Inventory		$
Other current assets		$ _____
TOTAL CURRENT ASSETS	(A)	$ _____

Fixed Assets

Property owned		$
Furniture and equipment		$
Business automobile		$
Leasehold improvements		$
Other fixed assets		$ _____
TOTAL FIXED ASSETS	(B)	$ _____
TOTAL ASSETS	(A+B = X)	$ _____

LIABILITIES

Current Liabilities (due within the next 12 months)

Bank loans		$
Other loans		$
Accounts payable		$
Other current liabilities		$ _____
TOTAL CURRENT LIABILITIES	(C)	$ _____

Long-term Liabilities

Mortgages		$
Long-term loans		$
Other long-term liabilities		$ _____
TOTAL LONG-TERM LIABILITIES	(D)	$ _____
TOTAL LIABILITIES	(C+D = Y)	$ _____
NET WORTH	(X-Y = Z)	$ _____
TOTAL NET WORTH AND LIABILITIES	(Y+Z)	$ _____

Figure II

Business Income and Expense Forecast for the Next 12 Months

One year estimate ending _____, 19 _____

Projected Number of Clients

For your services   _____

For your products   _____

TOTAL NUMBER OF CLIENTS   _____

Projected Income

Sessions $ _____

Product sales $ _____

Other $ _____

TOTAL INCOME $ _____

Projected Expenses

Start-up costs $ _____

Monthly expenses (x 12) $ _____

Annual expenses $ _____

TOTAL EXPENSES $ _____

TOTAL OPERATING PROFIT (OR LOSS) $ _____

CAPITAL REQUIRED FOR THE NEXT 12 MONTHS $ _____

Fish Farming Business

Start-Up Costs Worksheet	
Item	**Estimated Expense**
Open checking account	$
Telephone installation	$
Equipment	$
First & last month's rent, security deposit, etc.	$
Supplies	$
Business cards, stationery, etc.	$
Advertising and promotion package	$
Decorating and remodeling	$
Furniture and fixtures	$
Legal and professional fees	$
Insurance	$
Utility deposits	$
Beginning inventory	$
Installation of fixtures and equipment	$
Licenses and permits	$
Other	$
TOTAL	$

Fixed Annual Expense Worksheet	
Item	**Estimated Expense**
Property insurance	$
Business auto insurance	$
Licenses and permits	$
Liability insurance	$
Disability insurance	$
Professional society membership	$
Fees (legal, accounting, etc.)	$
Taxes	$
Other	$
TOTAL	$

Monthly Business Expense Worksheet		
Expense	**Estimated Monthly Cost**	**X 12**
Rent	$	$
Utilities	$	$
Telephone	$	$
Bank fees	$	$
Supplies	$	$
Stationery and business cards	$	$
Networking club dues	$	$
Education (seminars, books professional journals, etc.)	$	$
Business car (Payments, gas, repairs, etc)	$	$
Advertising and promotion	$	$
Postage	$	$
Entertainment	$	$
Repair, cleaning and maintenance	$	$
Travel	$	$
Business loan payments	$	$
Salary/Draw	$	$
Staff salaries	$	$
Miscellaneous	$	$
Taxes	$	$
Professional fees	$	$
Decorations	$	$
Furniture and fixtures	$	$
Equipment	$	$
Inventory	$	$
Other	$	$
TOTAL MONTHLY	$	$
TOTAL YEARLY		$

Cash Flow Forecast						
	January Estimate	January Actual	February Estimate	February Actual	March Estimate	March Actual
Beginning cash						
Plus monthly income from: Fees						
Sales						
Loans						
Other						
TOTAL CASH AND INCOME						
Expenses:						
Rent						
Utilities						
Telephone						
Bank fees						
Supplies						
Stationery and business cards						
Insurance						
Dues						
Education						
Auto						
Advertising and promotion						
Postage						
Entertainment						

	January Estimate	January Actual	February Estimate	February Actual	March Estimate	March Actual
Cash Flow Forecast (Continued)						
Repair and maintenance						
Travel						
Business loan payments						
Licenses and permits						
Salary/Draw						
Staff salaries						
Taxes						
Professional fees						
Decorations						
Furniture and fixtures						
Equipment						
Inventory						
Other Expenses						
TOTAL EXPENSES						
ENDING CASH (+/-)						

Notes _____

Chapter 6

Fish Farming Business Planning

Introduction

Our increasingly service oriented economy offers a widening spectrum of opportunities for customized and personalized small business growth. Though untrained entrepreneurs have traditionally had a high rate of failure, small businesses can be profitable. Success in a small Fish Farming business is not an accident. It requires both skills in a service or product area and acquisition of management and attitudinal competencies.

The purpose of this publication is to help you take stock of your interests, aptitudes and skills. Many people have good business ideas but not everyone has what it takes to succeed. If you are convinced that a profitable Fish Farming business is attainable, this publication will provide step-by-step guidance in development of the basic written business plan.

Information Gathering

A helpful tool for use in determining if you are ready to take the risks of an Fish Farming business operation is the SMA publication entitled *Going Into Business* (MP-12).

It will help you focus on the basic steps in information gathering and business planning.

Careful planning is required to research legal and tax issues, proper space utilization and to establish time management discipline. Inadequate or careless attention to development of a detailed business plan can be costly for you and your family in terms of lost time, wasted talent and disappearing dollars.

The Entrepreneurial Personality

A variety of experts have documented research that indicates that successful small business entrepreneurs have some common characteristics. How do you measure up? On this checklist, write a "Y" if you believe the statement describes you; a "N" if it doesn't; and a "U" if you can't decide:

_____ I have a strong desire to be my own boss.

_____ Win lose or draw, I want to be master of my own financial destiny.

_____ I have significant specialized business ability based on both my education and my experience.

_____ I have an ability to conceptualize the whole of a business; not just its individual parts, but how they relate to each other.

_____ I develop an inherent sense of what is "right" for a business and have the courage to pursue it.

_____ One or both of my parents were entrepreneurs; calculate risk-taking runs in the family.

_____ My life is characterized by a willingness and capacity to preserver.

_____ I possess a high level of energy, sustainable over long hours to make the business successful.

While not every successful Fish Farming business owner starts with a "Y" answer to all of these questions, three or four "N"s and "U"s should be sufficient reason for you to stop and give a second thought to going it alone. Many proprietors who sense entrepreneurial deficiencies seek extra training a support their limitations with help from a skilled team of business advisors such as accountants, bankers and attorneys.

Selecting a Business

A logical first step for the undecided is to list potential areas of personal background, special training, education and job experience, and special interests that could be developed into a business. Review the following list of activities which have proven marketable for others. On a scale of "0" (no interest or strength) to "10" (maximum interest or strength) indicate the potential for you and a total score for each activity.

Time Management

For both the novice and the experienced business person planning a small Fish Farming enterprise, an early concern requiring self-evaluation is time management.

It is very difficult for some people to make and keep work schedules even in a disciplined office setting. As your own boss the problem can be much greater. To determine how much time you can devote to your business, begin by drafting a weekly task timetable listing all current and potential responsibilities and the blocks of time required for each. When and how can business responsibilities be added without undue physical or mental stress on you or your family? Potential conflicts must be faced and resolved at the outset and as they occur, otherwise your business can become a nightmare. During the first year of operation, continue to chart, post and checkoff tasks on a daily, weekly and monthly basis.

Distractions and excuses for procrastination abound. It is important to keep both a planning and operating log. These tools will help avoid oversights and provide vital information when memory fails.

To improve the quality of work time, consider installation of a telephone line for the business and attaching an answering machine to take messages when you do not wish to be distracted or are away from your business. A business line has the added advantage of allowing you to have a business listing in the phone book and if you wish to buy it, an ad in the classified directory.

Is an Fish Farming Business Site Allowable?

Now you will want to investigate potential legal and community problems associated with operating the business. You should gather, read and digest specialized information concerning federal, state, county and municipal laws and regulations concerning Fish Farming business operations.

Check first! Get the facts in writing. Keep a topical file for future reference. Some facts and forms will be needed for your business plan. There may be limitations enforced that can make your planned business impossible or require expensive modifications to your property.

Items to be investigated, recorded and studied are:

TO DO   DONE

_____   _____   county or city zoning code restrictions

_____   _____   necessary permits and licenses for operation

_____   _____   state and local laws and codes regarding zoning

_____   _____   deed or lease restrictions such as covenants and restrictive conditions of purchase

_____	_____	parking and customer access; deliveries
_____	_____	sanitation, traffic and noise codes
_____	_____	signs and advertising
_____	_____	state and federal code requirements for space, ventilation, heat and light
_____	_____	limitations on the number and type of workers. If not, check with the local Chamber of Commerce office
_____	_____	reservations that neighbors may have about a business next to or near them

Here are some ways to collect your information. Call or visit the zoning office at county headquarters or city hall. In some localities the city or county Office of Economic Development has print materials available to pinpoint key "code" items affecting a business.

Even in rural areas, the era of unlimited free enterprise is over. Although the decision makers may be in the state capital or in a distant regional office of a federal agency, check before investing in inventory, equipment or marketing programs. If in doubt, call the state office of Industrial Development or the nearest SBA district office. In some states the county agent or home demonstration agent will have helpful information concerning rural or farm business development.

Is the Business Site Insurable?

In addition to community investigations, contact your insurance company or agent. It is almost certain that significant changes will be required in your coverage and limits when you start a business. When you have written a good description of your business, call your agent for help in insuring you properly against new hazards resulting from your business operations such as:

- Fire, theft and casualty damage to inventories and equipment
- business interruption coverage
- fidelity bonds for employees
- liability for customers, vendors and others visiting the business
- workmen's compensation
- group health and life insurance
- product liability coverage if you make or sell a product; workmanship liability for services
- business use of vehicle coverage

Overall Fish Farming Site Evaluation

After you have gathered as much information as seems practical you may wish to evaluate several different locations. Here's a handy checklist. Using the "0" to "10" scale, grade these vital factors:

Factors to Consider

Factor   **Grades 0-10**

1. Customer convenience   _____

2. Availability of merchandise or raw materials   _____

3. Nearby competition   _____

4. Transportation availability and rates   _____

5. Quality and quantity of employees available   _____

6. Availability of parking facilities   _____

7. Adequacy of utilities (sewer, water, power, gas)   _____

8. Traffic flow   _____

9. Tax burden   _____

10. Quality of police and fire services   _____

11. Environmental factors   _____

12. Physical suitability for future expansion   _____

13. Provision for future expansion   _____

14. Vendor delivery access   _____

15. Personal convenience   _____

16. Cost of operation   _____

17. Other factors including how big you get without moving _____

TOTALS   _____

Writing the Business Plan

Now that your research and plan development is nearing completion, it is time to move into action. If you are still in favor of going ahead, it is time to take several specific steps. The key one is to organize your dream scheme into a business plan.

What is it?

- As a business plan it is written by the Fish Farming business owner with outside help as needed
- It is accurate and concise as a result of careful study
- It explains how the business will function in the marketplace
- It clearly depicts its operational characteristics
- It details how it will be financed
- It outlines how it will be managed
- It is the management and financial "blueprint" for start-up and profitable operation
- It serves as a prospectus for potential investors and lenders

Why create it?

- The process of putting the business plan together, including the thought that you put in before writing it, forces you to take an objective, critical, unemotional look at your entire business proposal
- The finished written plan is an operational tool which, when properly used, will help you manage your business and work toward its success
- The completed business plan is a means for communicating your ideas to others and provides the basis for financing your business

Who should write it?

- The Fish Farming owner to the extend possible
- Seek assistance in weak areas, such as:
  - accounting
  - insurance
  - capital requirements
  - operational forecasting
  - tax and legal requirements

When should a business plan be used?

- To make crucial start-up decisions
- To reassure lenders or backers
- To measure operations progress
- To test planning assumptions
- As a basis for adjusting forecasts
- To anticipate ongoing capital and cash requirements
- As the benchmark for good operations management

Proposed Outline for Fish Farming Business Plan

This outline is suggested for a small proprietorship or family business. Shape it to fit *your* unique needs. For more complex manufacturing or franchise operations see the Resource section for other options.

Part I - Business Organization

Cover page:

    A.   Business name:

            Street address:

            Mailing address:

            Telephone number:

            Owner(s) name(s):

Inside pages:

    B.   Business form:

            (proprietorship, partnership, corporation)

            If incorporated (state incorporation)

            Include copies of key subsidiary documents in an appendix.

Remember even partnerships require written agreements of terms and conditions to avoid later conflicts and to establish legal entities and equities. Corporations require charters, articles of incorporation and bylaws.

Part II - Business Purpose and Function

In this section, write an accurate yet, concise description of the business. Describe the business you plan to start in narrative form.

What is the principal activity? Be specific. Give product or service description(s):

- retail sales?

- manufacturing?

- service?

- other?

How will it be started?

- a new start up

- the expansion of an existing business

- purchase of a going business

- a franchise operation

- actual or projected start up date

Why will it succeed? Promote your idea!

- how and why this business will be successful

- what is unique about your business

- what is its market "niche"

What is your experience in this business? If you have a current resume of your career, include it in an appendix and reference it here. Otherwise write a narrative here and include a resume in the finished product. If you lack specific experience, detail how you plan to gain it, such as training, apprenticeship or working with partners who have experience.

The Marketing Plan

The marketing plan is the core of your business rationale. To develop a consistent sales growth an Fish Farming business person much become knowledgeable about the market. To demonstrate your understanding, this section of the Fish Farming business plan should seek to concisely answer several basic questions:

Who is your market?

- Describe the profile of your typical customer
  Age?
  Male, female, both?
  How many in family?
  Annual family income?
  Location?
  Buying patterns?
  Reason to buy from you?

Other?

- Biographically describe your trading area (i.e., county, state, national)

- Economically describe your trading area: (single family, average earnings, number of children)

How large is the market?

- Total units or dollars?

- Growing _____ Steadily _____ Decreasing _____

- If growing, annual growth rate. _____

Who is your competition?

No small business operates in a vacuum. Get to know and respect the competition. Target your marketing plans. Identify direct competitors (both in terms of geography and product lines), and those who are similar or marginally comparative. Begin by listing names, addresses and products or service. Detail briefly but concisely the following information concerning each of your competitors:

- Who are the nearest ones?

- How are their businesses similar or competitive to yours?

- Do you have a unique "niche"? Describe it.

- How will your service or product be better or more saleable than your competitors?

- Are their businesses growing? Stable? Declining? Why?

- What can be learned from observing their operations or talking to their present or former clients?

- Will you have competitive advantages or disadvantages? Be honest!

What percent of the market will you penetrate?

1. estimate the market in total units or dollars

2. estimate your planned volume

3. amount your volume will add to total market

4. subtract 3 from 2

Item 4 represents the amount of your planned volume that must be taken away from the competition.

What pricing and sales terms are you planning?

The primary consideration in pricing a product or service is the value that it represents to the customer. If, on the previous checklist of features, your product is truly ahead of the field, you can command a premium price. On the other hand, if it is a "me too" product, you may have to "buy" a share of the market to get your foothold and then try to move price up later. This is always risky and difficult. One rule will always hold: ultimately, the market will set the price. If your selling price does not exceed your costs and expenses by the margin necessary to keep your business healthy, you will fail. Know your competitors pricing policies. Send a friend to comparison shop. Is there discounting? Special sales? Price leaders? Make some "blind" phone calls. Detail your pricing policy.

What is your sales plan?

Describe how you will sell, distribute or service what you sell. Be specific. Below are outlined some common practices:

Direct Sales - by telephone or in person. The tremendous growth of individual sales representatives who sell by party bookings, door to door, and through distribution of call back promotional campaigns suggests that careful research is required to be profitable.

Mail Order - Specialized markets for leisure time or unique products have grown as more two income families find less time to shop. Be aware of recent mail order legislation and regulation.

Franchising -

a. You may decide to either buy into someone else's franchise as a franchisee, or

b. Create your own franchise operation that sells rights to specific territories or product lines to others. Each will require further legal, financial and marketing research.

Management Plan

Who will do what?

Be sure to include four basic sets of information:

1. State a personal history of principals and related work, hobby or volunteer experience (include formal resumes in Appendix)

2. List and describe specific duties and responsibilities of each

3. List benefits and other forms of compensation for each

4. Identify other professional resources available to the business: Example: Accountant, lawyer, insurance broker, banker. Describe relationship of each to business: Example "Accountant available on part-time hourly basis, as needed, initial agreement calls for services not to exceed x hours per month at $xx.xx per hour."

To make this section graphically clear, start with a simple organizational chart that lists specific tasks and shows, *who* (type of person is more important than an individual name other than for principals) will do *what* indicate by arrows, work flow and lines of responsibility and/or communications. Consider the following examples:

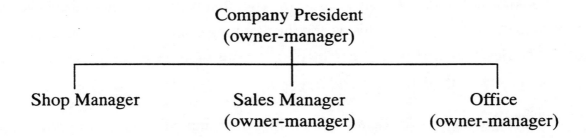

or like this?

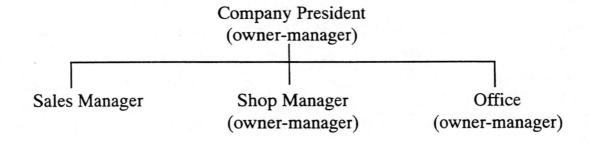

As the service business grows, its organization chart could look like this:

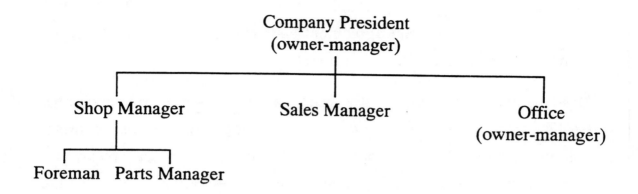

The Financial Plan

Clearly the most critical section of your business plan document is the financial plan. In formulating this part of the planning document, you will establish vital schedules that will guide the financial health of your business through the troubled waters of the first year and beyond.

Before going into the details of building the financial plan, it is important to realize that some basic knowledge of accounting is essential to the productive management of your business. If you are like most business owners, you probably have a deep and abiding interest in the product or services that you sell or intend to sell. You like to do what you do, and it is even more fulfilling that you are making money doing it. There is nothing wrong with that. Your conviction that what you are doing or making is worthwhile is vitally important to success. Nonetheless, the income of a coach who takes the greatest pride in producing a winning team will largely depend on someone keeping score of the wins and losses.

The business owner is no different. Your product or service may improve the condition of mankind for generations to come, but, unless you have access to an unlimited bankroll, you will fail if you don't make a profit. If you don't know what's going on in your business, you are not in a very good position to assure its profitability.

Most Fish Farming businesses will use the "cash" method of accounting with a system of record keeping that may be little more than a carefully annotated checkbook in which is recorded all receipts and all expenditures, backed up by a few forms of original entry (invoices, receipts, cash tickets). For a Sole Partnership, the business form assumed by this Management Aid, the very minimum of recorded information is that required to accurately complete the Federal Internal Revenue Service Form 1040, Schedule C. Other business types (partnerships, joint ventures, corporations) have similar requirements but use different tax forms.

If your business is, or will be, larger than just a small supplement to family income, you will need something more sophisticated. Stationery stores can provide you with several packaged small business account systems complete with simple journals and ledgers and detailed instructions in understandable language.

Should you feel that your accounting knowledge is so rudimentary that you will need professional assistance to establish your accounting system, the classified section of your telephone directory can lead you to a number of small business services that offer a complete range of accounting services. You can buy as much as you need, from a simple "pegboard" system all the way to computerized accounting, tax return service and monthly profitability consultation. Rates are reasonable for the services rendered and an investigative consultation will usually be free. Look under the heading, "Business Consultants," and make some calls.

Let's start by looking at the makeup of the financial plan for the business.

The Financial plan includes the following:

1. Financial Planning Assumptions - these are short statements of the conditions under which you plan to operate.

- Market health
- Date of start-up
- Sales build-up ($)
- Gross profit margin
- Equipment, furniture and fixtures required
- Payroll and other key expenses that will impact the financial plan

2. Operations Plan - Profit and Loss Projection - this is prepared for the first year's Budget. Appendix A-11.

3. Source of Funds Schedule - this shows the source(s) of your funds to capitalize the business and how they will be distributed among your fixed assets and working capital.

4. Pro Forma Balance Sheet - "Pro forma" refers to the fact that the balance sheet is before the fact, not actual. This form displays Assets, Liabilities and Equity of the business. This will indicate how much Investment will be required by the business and how much of it will be used as Working Capital in its operation.

5. Cash Flow Projection - this will forecast the flow of cash into and out of your business through the year. It helps you plan for staged purchasing, high volume months and slow periods.

Creating the Profit and Loss Projection.

Appendix A-11. Create a wide sheet of analysis paper with a three inch wide column at the extreme left and thirteen narrow columns across the page. Write at the top of the first page the planned name of your business. On the second line of the heading, write "Profit and Loss Projection." On the third line, write "First Year."

Then, note the headings on Appendix A-11 and copy them onto your 12-column sheet, copy the headings from the similar area on Exhibit A. Then follow the example set by Appendix A-11 and list all of the other components of your income, cost and expense structure. You may add or delete specific loans of expense to suit your business plan. Guard against consolidating too many types of expenses under one account lest you lose control of the components. At the same time, don't try to break down expenses so discretely that accounting becomes a nuisance instead of a management tool. Once again, Exhibit A provides ample detail for most businesses.

Now, in the small column just to the left of the first monthly column, you will want to note which of the items in the left-hand column are to be estimated on a monthly (M) or yearly (Y) basis. Items such as Sales, Cost of Sales and Variable expenses will be estimated monthly based on planned volume and seasonal or other estimated fluctuations. Fixed Expenses can usually be estimated on a yearly basis and divided by twelve to arrive at even monthly values. The "M" and "Y" designations will be used later to distinguish between variable and fixed expense.

Depreciation allowances for Fixed Assets such as production equipment, office furniture and machines, vehicles, etc. will be calculated from the Source of Funds Schedule.

Appendix A-11 describes line by line how the values on the Profit and Loss Projection are developed. Use this as your guide.

Source of Funds Schedule

To create this schedule, you will need to create a list of all the Assets that you intend to use in your business, how much investment each will require and the source of funds to capitalize them. A sample of such a list is shown below:

51

Asset	Cost	Source of Funds
Cash	$2,500	Personal savings
Accounts Receivable	3,000	From profits
Inventory	2,000	Vendor credit
Pickup truck	5,000	Currently owned
Packaging machine	10,000	Installment purchase
Office desk and chair	300	Currently owned
Calculator	75	Personal cash
Electric typewriter*	500	Personal savings

* A note about office equipment, test use or rent two or more brands that appear to meet your needs and select the one with which you feel most comfortable. Don't be afraid to ask others who have had to make this decision for advice. Compatibility of your system with those of potential typesetting services or printers should be of high considerations. If you are not quite sure, consider renting or leasing the equipment until you are. Service contracts on such complex electronic gear are usually a good insurance policy.

Before you leave your Source of Funds Schedule, indicate the number of months (years x 12) of useful life for depreciable fixed assets. (An example, the pickup truck, the packaging machine and the furniture and office equipment would be depreciable.) Generally, any individual item of equipment, furniture, fixtures, vehicles, etc., costing over $100 should be depreciated. For more information on allowances for depreciation, you can get free publications and assistance from your local Internal Revenue Service office. Divided the cost of each fixed asset item by the number or months over which it will be depreciated. You will need this data to enter as monthly depreciation on your Profit and Loss Projection. All of the data on the Source of Funds Schedule will be needed to create the Balance Sheet.

Creating the Pro Forma Balance Sheet

Appendix A-13. This is the Balance Sheet Form. There are a number of variations of this form and you may find it prudent to ask your banker for the form that the bank uses for small business. It will make it easier for them to evaluate the health of your business. Use this to get started and transfer the data to your preferred form later. Accompanying Appendix A-12 which describes line by line how to develop the Balance Sheet.

Even though you may plan to stage the purchase of some assets through the year, for the purpose of this pro forma Balance Sheet, assume that all assets will be provided at the start-up.

Cash Flow Projection

An important subsidiary schedule to your financial plan is a monthly Cash Flow Projection. Prudent business management practice is to keep no more cash in the business than is needed to operate it and to protect it from catastrophe. In most small businesses, the problem is rarely one of having too much cash. A Cash Flow Projection is made to advise management of the amount of cash that is going to be absorbed by the operation of the business and compares it against the amount that will be available.

SBA has created an excellent form for this purpose and it is shown as Appendix B. Your projection should be prepared on 13-column analysis paper to allow for a twelve-month projection. Appendix B represents a line by line description and explanation of the components of the Cash Flow Projection which provides a step-by-step method of preparation.

Resources

U.S. Small Business Administration
Office of Business Development

Business Development Publication
MP15

Fish Farming
Business Associations for the Entrepreneur

Catfish Farmers of America (CFA)
1100 Hwy. 82 E
Indianola, MS 38751
Hugh Warren, Exec. VP
PH: (601) 887-2699   FX: (601) 887-6857
Founded: 1966   Members: 400

Florida Tropical Fish Farms Association (FTFFA)
P.O. Drawer 1519
Winter Haven, FL 33880
David Boozer, Exec. Dir
PH: (813) 293-5710   FX: (813) 299-5154
Founded: 1984   Members: 330

International Aquaculture Foundation (IAF)
2440 Virginia Ave. NW, No. D 305
Washington, DC 20037
PH: (202) 785-8215
Founded: 1984   Members: 5

Notes _____

Chapter 7

Managing The Business

Delegating work, responsibility, and authority is difficult in a small business because it means letting others make decisions which involved spending the owner/manager's money. At a minimum, he should delegate enough authority to get the work done, to allow assistants to take initiative, and to keep the operation moving in his absence. Coaching those who carry responsibility and authority in self-improvement is essential and emphasis in allowing competent assistants to perform in their own style rather than insisting that things be done exactly as the owner/manager would personally do them is important. "Let others take care of the details" is the meaning of delegating work and responsibility. In theory, the same principles for getting work done through other people apply whether you have 25 employees and one top assistant or 150 to 200 employees and several keymen yet, putting the principles into practice is often difficult.

Delegation is perhaps the hardest job owner/managers have to learn. Some never do. They insist on handling many details and work themselves into early graves. Others pay lip service to the idea but actually run a one-man shop. They give their assistants many responsibilities but little or no authority. Authority is the fuel that makes the machine go when you delegate word and responsibility. If an owner/manager is to run a successful company, he must delegate authority properly. How much authority is proper depends on your situation. At a minimum, you should delegate enough authority: (1) to get the work done, (2) to allow keymen to take initiative, (3) to keep things going in your absence.

The person who fills a key management spot in the organization must either be a manager or be capable of becoming one. A manager's chief job is to plan, direct, and coordinate the work of others. He should possess the three "I's" — Initiative, Interest, and Imagination. The manager of a department must have enough self-drive to start and keep things moving. Personality traits must be considered. A keyman should be strong-willed enough to overcome opposition when necessary.

When you manage through others, it is essential that you keep control. You do it by holding a subordinate responsible for his actions and checking the results of those actions. In controlling your assistants, try to strike a balance. You should not get into a keyman's operations so closely that you are "in his hair" nor should you be so far removed that you lose control of things.

You need feedback to keep yourself informed. Reports provide a way to get the right kind of feedback at the right time. This can be daily, weekly, or monthly depending on how soon you need the information. Each department head can report his progress, or lack of it, in the unit of production that is appropriate for his activity; for example, items packed in the shipping room, sales per territory, hours of work per employee.

For the owner/manager, delegation does not end with good control. It involves coaching as well, because management ability is not required automatically. You have to teach it. Just as important, you have to keep your managers informed just as you would be if you were doing their jobs.

Part of your job is to see that they get the facts they need for making their decisions. You should be certain that you convey your thinking when you coach your assistants. Sometimes words can be inconsistent with thoughts. Ask questions to make sure that the listener understands your meaning. In other words, delegation can only be effective when you have good communications.

Sometimes an owner/manager finds himself involved in many operational details even though he does everything that is necessary for delegation of responsibility. In spite of defining authority, delegation, keeping control, and coaching, he is still burdened with detailed work. Usually, he had failed to do one vital thing. He has refused to stand back and let the wheels turn.

If the owner/manager is to make delegation work, he must allow his subordinates freedom to do things their way. He and the company are in trouble if he tries to measure his assistants by whether they do a particular task exactly as he would do it. They should be judged by their results — not their methods. No two persons react exactly the same in every situation. Be prepared to see some action taken differently from the way in which you would do it even though your policies are well defined. Of course, if an assistant strays too far from policy, you need to bring him back in line. You cannot afford second-guessing.

You should also keep in mind that when an owner/manager second-guesses his assistants, he risks destroying their self-confidence. If the assistant does not run his department to your satisfaction and if his shortcomings cannot be overcome, then replace him. But when results prove his effectiveness, it is good practice to avoid picking at each move he makes.

Notes _____

Chapter 8

Business Resource Information

Books
Finding Your Niche, by Lawrence J. Pino. 1994, Berkley Publishing Group, New York

Finding Your Perfect Work: The New Career Guide to Making a Living, Creating a Life,
by Paul and Sarah Edwards. 1996 J.P. Tarcher, Los Angeles, CA.

The Pathfinder: How to Choose or Change Your Career for a Lifetime of Satisfaction and Success, by Nicholas Lore. 1997, Fireside, New York.

Which Business? Help in Selecting Your New Venture,
by Nancy Drescher. 1997, Oasis Press, Grants Pass, OR.

Books for Start-Up Business
Anatomy of a Business Plan, 3rd ed.,
by Linda Pinson and Jerry Jinnett. 1996, Upstart Publishing Company, Dover, NH.

How to Write a Successful Business Plan,
by Jerre Lewis and Leslie Renn. 1997, Lewis & Renn Assocs., 10315 Harmony Dr.,
Interlochen, MI 49643. $14.95 + $3 postage and handling.

Growing Your Home-Based Business,
by Kim T. Gordon. 1992, Prentice Hall, Upper Saddle River, NJ.

Surefire Strategies for Growing Your Home-Based Business,
by David Schaefer. 1997, Dearborn Trade, Chicago, IL.

Your First Business: How to Really Start Your Own Business This Year, by Mainstay Company.
1997, 511 Avenue of the Americas, Suite 350, New York, NY 10011-8436. Send $19.95
(includes postage and handling) by check or money order.

Books for Financing Businesses

Launching Your Home-Based Business: How to Successfully Plan, Finance, and Grow Your New Venture, by David H. Bangs, Jr. 1997, Dearborn Trade, Chicago, IL.

Minding Her Own Business: The Self-Employed Woman's Guide to Taxes and Record keeping by Jan Zobel. 1998, Easthill Press, Oakland, CA.

Small Business Financial Resource Guide (booklet). Write to: The National Federation of Independent Business (NFIB), 600 Maryland Ave., SW, #700, Washington, DC 20024. <http://www.nfibonline.com>

Books for Internet Sites

Cheapskate's Guide to Building a Web Site with Windows 95/NT, by Pete Palmer. 1998, Prentice Hall Professional, Upper Saddle River, NJ.

Books on Legal Structure for Businesses

Choosing a Legal Structure for Your Business, by Stuart A. Handmaker. 1997, Prentice Hall Trade, Upper Saddle River, NJ.

Business Plan Guide

Entrepreneur's Business Guide, Writing an Effective Business Plan. (800) 421-2300. $69 + shipping and handling.

Business Plan Software

Palo Alto Software, 144 East 14th Avenue, Eugene, OR 97401 (888) 752-6776 <http://www.palo-alto.com/>

Microsoft Corporation, Redmond, WA 98052 (800) 426-9400; <http://www.microsoft.com>

Arden, Lynie, The Work at Home Source Book. Boulder, CO: Live Oak Publications, 1996.

Bautista, Veltisezar. How to Build a Successful One-Person Business. Farmington Hills, MI: Bookhaus Publishers, 1995.

Liraz Publishing. The Entrepreneur Test. The Managing a Small Business CD-ROM: Liraz Publishing Co., 1996.

Liraz, Publishing. The 30 Best Inspiring Anecdotes of All Times. The Managing a Small Business CD-ROM: Liraz Publishing Co., 1996.

Lord, David. National Business Employment Weekly Guide to Self-Employment. New York: John Wiley and Sons, 1996.

Ramsey, Dan. 101 Best Weekend Businesses. Franklin Lakes, NJ: Career Press, 1996.

Government Resources - Federal
Bureau of the Census, Customer Services
Data User Services Division
Suitland and Silver Hill roads, Washington, DC 20233
(301) 763-8576; <http://www.census.gov>
Provides statistics

Bureau of Labor Statistics
(202) 606-6378
<http://www.bls.gov>
Also provides statistics

Consumer Information Center
P.O. Box 100 Pueblo, CO 81002
<http://www.peublo.gsa.gov>
Send for free Consumer Information Catalog. You can order free or low cost information on many topics, including small business information.

Internal Revenue Service
4300 Caroline Ave., Richmond, VA 23222
(800) 829-1040
<http://.www.securetax.com>, <http://www.irs.ustreas.gov> (other state and federal tax forms)

Office of Women's Business Ownership
Small Business Administration
409 Third St. SW, 6th Floor, Washington, DC 20416
(202) 205-6673; <http://www/sba/gov/womenbusiness
Send for a free packet of business information of interest to women.

Service Corps of Retired Executives Association (SCORE)
409 Third St., SW, 4th Floor, Washington, DC 20024
<http://www.sba.gov/SCORE/program.html>
A nonprofit association funded by the SBA, made up of mostly retired men and women who
worked in business management. Services are free and they provide small business counselin
Write for SCORE contacts in your area or call your local SBDC.

U.S. Patent and Trademark Office
Washington, DC 20231
(703) 308-HELP [4357]; <http://uspto.gov>

U.S. Small Business Administration (SBA)
409 Third St., SW, Washington, DC 20416
This is the primary source for government assistance for small businesses. Their regional and
Small Business Development Centers offer free or low-cost assistance, seminars, and
workshops. They also offer many helpful publications.

Helpful Resource Book/Directories
    These can usually be found in college or larger public libraries.

2001 Sources for Financing a Small Business
    Book of Business Plans; National Directory of Women-Owned Firms;
    Small Business Sourcebook, Gale Research.

Directory of Directories, Gale Research, Detroit, MI.
    Dun's Business Rankings

Internet Business 500: The Top Essential Sites for Business, by Ryan Bernard.
    1995, Ventana Communications Group, Inc., Research Triangle Park, NC.

Thomas's Lists of Manufacturers, <http://www/thomasregister.com>

U.S. Industrial Outlook
    See also *A Directory of National Women's Organizations* published by:
    The National Council for Research on Women
    The Sara Delano Roosevelt Memorial House
    47-49 E. 65th St.
    New York, NY 10021

A Concise Guide
To Starting Your
Own Business

Page A-2

Guide Overview

A concise overview of the complete guide to starting and operating a successful business.

The following topics are presented:

- Business Plan for Small Businesses.
- Getting Started
- Deciding Where To Start The Business
- Business Patronage Statistics
- Site Location
- Site Selection Criteria — Some General Questions.
- Choosing The Proper Method of Organization
- What Is A Corporation?
- Estimating Start-up Costs
- Preparing An Income Statement
- Preparing A Balance Sheet
- Marketing The Business
- Marketing Planning — An Outline for Marketing
- Advertising Media
- Management and Getting The Work Done
- Sample Organization Chart
- Summary of the Business Plan
- Guide Summary
- Reference Materials

Business Plan for Small Businesses

I. Type of Business

II. Location

III. Target Market

IV. Planning Process

V. Organizational Structure

VI. Staffing Procedures

VII. Control

VIII. Market Strategy

IX. Financial Planning

X. Budgeted Balance Sheet

XI. Budgeted Income Statement

XII. Budgeted Cash Flow Statement

XIII. Break-even Chart

Getting Started

Following is a list of what you need to accomplish to insure that your business endeavor will head in the right direction.

1. Define your educational background and work experience

2. Survey all basic types of businesses.

3. Define what type of business matches your experience and educational background.

4. Choose only the business that you would like to own and operate.

5. Define what products or services your business will be marketing.

6. Define who will be using your products/services.

7. Define why they will be purchasing your products/services.

8. List all competitors in your marketing area.

Deciding Where to Start the Business

Will your business fulfill a need in the area you plan to bring your business to? This section provides you with some important information you need to examine before taking your ideas any further:

1. Decide where you want to live.

2. Choose several areas that would match your priorities.

3. Use the list that follows as a guide to see if your location will match the estimated population needed to support your business. The numbers which follow the type of business indicate the typical number of inhabitants per year.

Business Patronage Statistics

Food Stores
Grocery Stores 1,534
Meat and Fish
(Sea Food) Markets . . . 17,876
Candy, Nut, and
Confectionery Stores . . 31,409
Retail Bakeries 12,563
Dairy Products Stores . . . 41,587

Eating and Drinking
Restaurant, Lunch Rooms . 1,583
Cafeterias 19,341
Refreshment Places 3,622
Drinking Places 2,414

General Merchandise
Variety Stores 10,373
General Merchandise 9,837

Apparel/Accessories Stores
Women's Ready-To-
Wear Stores 7,102
Women's Accessory and
Specialty Stores 25,824
Men's and Boy's Clothing
and Furnishings 11,832
Family Clothing 16,890
Shoe Stores 9,350

Furniture, Home Furnishings, and Equipment Stores
Furniture Stores 7,210
Floor Covering 29,543
Drapery, Curtains, and
Upholstery Stores 62,585
House, Appliances 12,485
Radios and TV's 20,346
Record Shops 112,144
Musical Instruments 46,332

Building Materials, Hardware, and Farm Equipment Dealers
Lumber and other Building
Materials Dealers 8,124
Paint, Glass, and Wallpaper
Stores 22,454
Hardware Stores 10,206
Farm Equipment Dealers . 14,793

Automotive Dealers
Motor Vehicle Dealers,
New and Used Cars 6,000
Motor Vehicle Dealers,
Used Cars only 17,160
Tire, battery, and
Accessory Dealers 8,800

Boat Dealers 61,500

Household Trailer Dealers . 44,746

Gasoline Service Stations . . . 1,395

Miscellaneous
Antique and Secondhand
Stores 17,170
Book and Stationery Stores 28,580
Drugstores 4,268
Florists 13,531
Fuel Oil Dealers 25,000
Garden Supply Stores . . . 65,000
Gift, Novelty Shops 26,000
Hobby, Toy, and Game
Shops 61,000
Jewelry Stores 13,400
Optical Goods Stores . . . 62,800
Sporting Goods Store 27,000

From *Starting and Managing a Small Business of Your Own, 1973;*
Small Business Administration, Washington, DC

Page A-6

Site Location

1. Define your number of inhabitants per store.

2. Locate several sites/locations that will match your inhabitants per stores.

3. Define population and its growth potential.

4. Define local ordinances and zoning regulations that you will need in order to start your type of business.

5. Define your trading area and all competitors in your trading area.

6. Define parking need, for your kind of business.

7. Define special needs, etc., lighting, heating, ventilation.

8. Define rental cost of site/location.

9. Define why customers will come to your site/location.

10. Define the future of your site/location as to population growth.

11. Define your space needs and match with site/location selection.

12. Define the image of your business and make sure it matches your site/location.

Site Selection Criteria — Some General Questions

- Is the site centrally located to reach my market?

- What is the transportation availability and what are the rates?

- What provisions for future expansion can I make:

- What is the topography of the site (slope and foundation)?

- What is the housing availability for workers and managers?

- What environmental factors (schools, cultural, community atmosphere) might affect my business and my employees?

- What will the quality of this site be in 5 years, 10 years, 25 years?

- What is my estimate of this site in relation to my major competitor?

- What other media are available for advertising? How many radio and television stations are there?

- Is the Quantity and quality of available labor concentrated in a given area in the city or town? If so, is commuting a way of living in that city or town?

- Is the city centrally located to my suppliers?

- What are the labor conditions, including such things as relationships with the business community and average wages and salaries paid?

- Is the local business climate healthy, or are business failures especially high in the area?

- What about tax requirements? Is there a city business tax? Income tax? What is the property tax rate? Is there a personal property tax? Are there other special taxes?

- Is the available police and fire protection adequate?

- Is the city or town basically well planned and managed in terms of such items as electric power, sewage, and paved streets and sidewalks?

Page A-8

Choosing the Proper Method of Organization

Listed below are legal forms of business available to the small business entrepreneur:

Sole Proprietorship

Advantages
- Simple to start
- All profits to owner
- Owner in direct control
- Easy entry and exit
- Taxed as individual

Disadvantages
- Unlimited liability
- "Jack-of-all-trades"
- Capital requirement limited
- Limited life
- Employee turn-over

Partnership

Advantages
- Easy to originate
- Credit rating
- Talent combination
- Legal Contract

Disadvantages
- Unlimited liability
- Misunderstandings
- Partner withdrawal
- Regulations

Corporation

Advantages
- Limited liability
- Expansion potential
- Transfer of ownership
- Retain employees

Disadvantages
- Double taxation
- Charter restrictions
- Employee motivation
- Legal regulations

What Is A Corporation?

A corporation is an artificial being, invisible, intangible, and existing only in contemplation of the law," wrote Chief Justice John Marshall. In other words, the corporation exists as a separate entity apart from its owners, the shareholders. It makes contracts; it is liable; it pays taxes. It is a "legal person".

The corporation is the most complex of the three major forms of business ownership. The corporation stands as a separate legal entity in the eyes of the law. The life of the corporation is independent of the owners' lives. Because the owners, called shareholders, are legally separate from the corporation, they can sell their interests in the business without affecting the continuation of the business. When a corporation is founded, it accepts the regulations and restrictions placed on it by the state in which it is incorporated and any other state in which it chooses to do business. Generally, the corporation must report its financial operations to the state's attorney general on an annual basis.

Page A-10

Estimating Start-up Costs

Item	Amount
Fixtures and Equipment	$ _____
Building & Land (If Needed)	_____
Store and/or Office Supplies	_____
Remodeling and Decorating	_____
Deposits on Utilities	_____
Insurance	_____
Installation of Fixtures	_____
Legal Fees	_____
Professional Fees	_____
Telephone	_____
Rental	_____
Salaries and Wages	_____
Inventory if Retailing	_____
Licenses and Permits	_____
Advertising and Promotion	_____
TOTAL Estimated Start-up Cost	$_____

Preparing An Income Statement

What is an Income Statement?

The income statement shows the income received and the expenses incurred over a period of time. Income received (sales) comes essentially from the sales of the merchandise or service which your business is formed to sell. Expenses incurred are the expired costs that have been incurred during the same period of time.

Plan A Budgeted Income Statement For One Year

1. Project Total Sales
2. Estimate Total Expenditures
3. Example Listed Below for Income Statement

Percents	1	2	3	4	5	6	7	8	9	10	11	12
Sales												
Cost of Sales												
Gross Profit												
Expenditure												
Rent Expense												
Supplies												
Wages/Salaries												
Utilities												
Insurance												
Depreciation												
Interest												
Miscellaneous												
Net Profit												

Preparing A Balance Sheet

What is a Balance Sheet?

The balance sheet shows the assets, liabilities and owner's net worth in a business as of a given date.

- Assets are the things owned by your business, including both physical things and claims against others.
- Liabilities are the amounts owned to others, the creditors of the firm.
- Net worth or owner's equity is the owner's claim to the assets after liabilities are accounted for.

A Budgeted Balance Sheet For One Year

- List all your business property at their cost to you: these are your assets.
- List all debts, or what your business owes on all your property; these are your liabilities.
- Take your total property balance (Assets), and subtract the total amount you owe (Liabilities).
- The balance is what you own in your business called (Owner's equity).
- Add Total Liabilities (2) & Total Owner's Equity (3).
- Listed on the next page is an example of a balance sheet.

NAME OF BUSINESS
BALANCE SHEET
DATE

ASSETS
Current Assets
  Cash
  Accounts Receivable   _____
Merchandise Inventories   _____
    TOTAL CURRENT ASSETS   _____

Fixed Assets
  Land
  Building   _____
  Equipment   _____
    TOTAL FIXED ASSETS   _____
      TOTAL ASSETS   1). _____

LIABILITIES
Current Liabilities
  Accounts Payable   _____
  Note Payable   _____
  Payroll Taxes Payable   _____
    TOTAL CURRENT LIABILITIES   _____

Long-term Liabilities
  Mortgage Payable   _____
  Long-term Note   _____
    TOTAL LONG-TERM LIABILITIES   _____
      TOTAL LIABILITIES   2). _____

OWNER'S EQUITY
Proprietor's Capital   3). _____

    TOTAL LIABILITIES & OWNER'S EQUITY   (2 &3). _____

Page A-14

Marketing The Business

1. Define Your Market
   - Type of Customers
   - Age, Income, Occupation of your customers
   - Type of Trading Area

2. Promotion of Your Business
   - Advertising
   - Setting your Image

3. Customer Policy Plan
   - Develop a Customer Profile
   - Customer Services
   - Customer Needs

4. Pricing Your Products/Services
   - Know all your Costs
   - Know your Profit Margin
   - Know Competitor's Price
   - Know what Return you want on your Investment

5. Sales Promotion
   - Coupons
   - Contests
   - Displays
   - Demonstrations
   - Giveaways
   - Banners

6. Public Relations
   - Newspaper Article
   - Contact Trade Association
   - Radio Promotion
   - TV Promotion

7. Segmentation of your Market
   - Age
   - Occupation
   - Income
   - Location
   - Education
   - Hobbies

Marketing Planning

Outline for Marketing

I. Product/Service Concept:
    a. Name of product or service
    b. Descriptive characteristics of product or service
    c. Unit sales
    d. Analysis of market trends

II. Number of Customers in your Market Area:
    a. Profile of customers
    b. Average customer expenditure
    c. Total market

III. Your Market Potential:
    a. Total market divided by competition
    b. Total market multiplied by percent who will buy your product

IV. Needs of Customers:
    a. Identification
    b. Pleasure
    c. Social approval
    d. Personal interest
    e. Price

V. Direct Marketing Sources:
    a. Trade magazines
    b. Trade associations
    c. Small Business Administration (SBA)
    d. Government Publications
    e. Yellow pages
    f. Marketing directories

VI Customer Profile:
    a. Geographical
    b. Gender
    c. Age range
    d. Income brackets
    e. Occupation
    f. Educational level

Advertising Media

Medium	Market Coverage	Type of Audience
Daily newspaper	Single community or entire metro area: zoned editions some-times available	General
Weekly newspaper	Single Community	Residents
Telephone Directory	Geographical area or occupational field served by the directory	Active shoppers for goods or services
Direct mail audience	Controlled by the advertiser	Controlled
Radio audience	Definable market area	Selected
Television audience	Definable market area surrounding TV Stations	Various
Outdoor	Entire metro area	General auto drivers
Magazine	Entire metro area or magazine region	Selected audience

Management and Getting the Work Done

1. Define your objective for starting your business.

2. Define your goals: profit growth for first three years.

3. Develop an organization chart of your business.

4. Define your personal needs.
   - Hiring proper employees
   - Training employees
   - Motivation

5. Define all responsibility for each person in your business.

6. Define all authority.
   - Who will hire and fire?
   - Who will select and train all personnel?
   - Who will keep the important records as to inventory, purchasing, sales records, cash records, etc.?

7. Define all laws and regulations that will be requirements for operating your business.

8. Review all duties and tasks with all your employees.

9. Write a summary of all the important tasks that you want to finish in your first year in business.

Sample Organization Chart

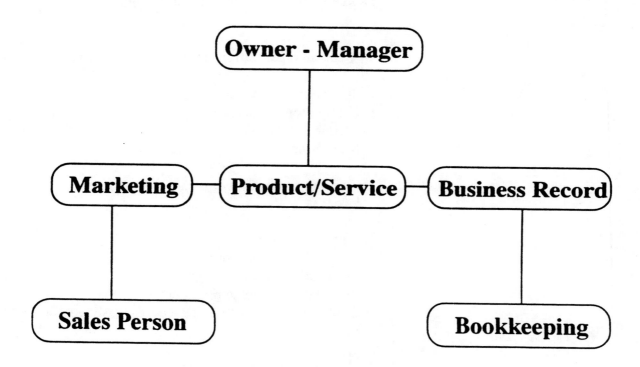

Summary of The Business Plan

Name of Business
BUSINESS PLAN
Date

1. Define your business
   * Name all principals
   * Address and phone number

2. Define your products or services

3. Define your market

4. Define your site or location

5. Advertising Plan
   * Budget
   * Media

6. Chart of Start-up cost

7. Worksheet of Income Statement
   * Revenue/Income
   * Expenses

8. Worksheet of Balance Sheet
   * Assets (Property)
   * Capital (Owner's Equity)
   * Liabilities (Debts)

9. Personnel Outline
   * Number of Employees
   * Staffing & Training

10. Management Organization
    * Organization Chart
    * Evaluation Policy
    * Job Profile

11. Special Statement
    * 3-Year Sales Schedule
    * Cash Flow
    * 3-Year Expense Schedule

Appendix A Summary

1. Contact your State Commerce Department for guidelines in starting your business.

2. Contact your City/County Clerk for guidelines in starting your business.

3. Contact all other Governmental Centers that will furnish you all the legal regulations and tax laws that will effect your business.
   - State Government
   - Internal Revenue Service
   - State Employment Security Commission
   - Department of Treasury
   - City Governmental Units

     a. Fire
     b. Police
     c. Zoning
     d. Building Permits
     e. Health
     f. Water & Sewage

4. Township Government
   - Local Legal Requirements
   - Local Taxes
   - Local Health Permits
   - Local Zoning Laws

Reference Materials

Management Aids Titles

Contact the

**Small Business Administration
P.O. Box 15434
Fort Worth, TX 76119**

for the following booklets:

- Number 2.025   Thinking About Going Into Business
- Number 2.010   Planning and Goal Setting For Business
- Number 1.016   Sound Cash Management
- Number 1.001   The A.B.C's. of Borrowing
- Number 1.008   Break-even Analysis
- Number 2.022   Business Plan For Service Firms
- Number 2.023   Business Plans for Retail Firms

Notes

Appendix B

HOUSEHOLD NEEDS

Many small business start-ups fail due to their inability to support their owners. Rarely do new businesses support their owners from the start. However, many individuals fail to recognize this fact. In addition, then, to a sound business plan, it is necessary for an owner to project the household cash needs month-by-month for the first three years of the business' operation. As a new business owner, you should be able to support yourself until your new business is able to support you in a manner to which you are accustomed.

MONTHLY HOUSEHOLD CASH NEEDS

Regular NON-BUSINESS Income
Spouse's salary _____
Investment income _____
Social security _____
Other income _____
Retirement benefits _____
Less taxes _____
Net monthly income ===========

Regular Monthly Expenses

Housing
Mortgage/Rent _____
Utilities _____
Homeowner's insurance _____
Property taxes _____
Home repairs _____

Living Expenses
Groceries _____
Telephone _____
Tuition _____
Transportation _____
Meals _____
Child care _____
Medical expenses _____
Clothing _____
Personal _____

Insurance Premiums
Life insurance _____
Disability insurance _____
Auto insurance _____
Medical insurance _____

Debt Repayment
Auto loans _____
Consumer debt _____

Discretionary Expenses
Entertainment _____
Vacation _____
Gifts _____
Retirement contributions _____
Investment savings _____
Charitable contributions _____
Dues, magazines, etc. _____
Professional fees _____
Other _____

Total Monthly Expenses ===========

Monthly Surplus/Deficit ===========

Total Year Surplus/Deficit ===========
(Monthly x 12)

Available Assets to Cover Deficit
Checking accounts _____
Savings accounts _____
Money market accounts _____
Personal credit lines _____
Marketable securities _____
Lump-sum retirement/
  severance _____
Other assets _____

Total Assets ===========

NEEDED RESERVES
  Total Assets-Deficit ===========

PERSONAL FINANCIAL STATEMENT

This is a picture of your personal financial condition to date. It is a very important part of any loan application and/or interview, especially when a loan for a projected new business is under consideration.

PERSONAL FINANCIAL STATEMENT

_____ _____ , 19 _____

Assets
Cash
Savings accounts
Stocks, bonds, other securities
Accounts/Notes receivable
Life insurance cash value
Rebates/Refunds
Autos/Other vehicles
Real estate
Vested pension plan/Retirement accounts
Other assets

TOTAL ASSETS $ _____

Liabilities

Accounts payable
Contracts payable
Notes payable
Taxes
Real estate loans
Other liabilities

TOTAL LIABILITIES $ _____

TOTAL ASSETS $ _____

LESS TOTAL LIABILITIES $ _____

NET WORTH $ _____

BALANCE SHEET

A balance sheet is a current financial statement. It is a dollars and cents description of your business (existing or projected) which lists all of its assets and liabilities.

BALANCE SHEET

_____ _____ , 19 _____

	YEAR 1	YEAR II
Current Assets		
Cash	_____	_____
Accounts receivable	_____	_____
Inventory	_____	_____
Fixed Assets		
Real estate	_____	_____
Fixtures and equipment	_____	_____
Vehicles	_____	_____
Other Assets		
License	_____	_____
Goodwill	_____	_____
TOTAL ASSETS	$_____	$_____
Current Liabilities		
Notes payable (due within 1 year)	$_____	$_____
Accounts payable	_____	_____
Accrued expenses	_____	_____
Taxes owed	_____	_____
Long-Term Liabilities		
Notes payable (due after 1 year)	_____	_____
Other	_____	_____
TOTAL LIABILITIES	$_____	$_____
NETWORTH (ASSETS minus LIABILITIES)	$_____	$_____

TOTAL LIABILITIES plus NET WORTH should equal ASSETS

PROFIT AND LOSS STATEMENT

A profit and loss statement is a detailed earnings statement for the previous full year (if you are already in business). Existing businesses are also required to show a profit and loss statement for the current period to the date of the balance sheet.

PROJECTED PROFIT AND LOSS STATEMENT

	Month 1	Month 2	Month 3	Month 4	Month 5	Month 6	Month 7	Month 8	Month 9	Month 10	Month 11	Month 12
Total Net Sales												
Cost of Sales												
GROSS PROFIT												
Controllable Expenses												
Salaries												
Payroll taxes												
Security												
Advertising												
Automobile												
Dues and subscriptions												
Legal and accounting												
Office supplies												
Telephone												
Utilities												
Miscellaneous												
Total Controllable Expenses												
Fixed Expenses Depreciation												
Insurance												
Rent												
Taxes and licenses												
Loan payments												
Total Fixed Expenses												
TOTAL EXPENSES												
NET PROFIT (LOSS) **(before taxes)**												

CASH FLOW PROJECTIONS

A cash flow projection is a forcast of the cash (checks or money orders) a business anticipates receiving and disbursing during the course of a month. Well managed, the cash flow should be sufficient to meet the cash requirements for the following month.

CASH FLOW PROJECTIONS

	Start-up or prior to loan	Month 1	Month 2	Month 3	Month 4	Month 5	Month 6	Month 7	Month 8	Month 9	Month 10	Month 11	Month 12	TOTAL
Cash (beginning of month														
Cash on hand														
Cash in bank														
Cash in investments														
Total Cash														
Income (during month)														
Cash sales														
Credit sales payment														
Investment income														
Loans														
Other cash income														
Total Income														
TOTAL CASH AND INCOME														
Expenses (during month														
Inventory or new material														
Wages (including owner's)														
Taxes														
Equipment expense														
Overhead														
Selling expense														
Transportation														
Loan repayment														
Other cash expenses														
TOTAL EXPENSES														
CASH FLOW EXCESS (end of month)														
CASH FLOW CUMULATIVE (Monthly)														

Getting Down to Business…

Fish Farming

**An Instructional Guide for Creating A Small Business
by Jerre G. Lewis, M.A.
& Leslie D. Renn, M.S.**

Notes _____

Water is crucial. High quality water must be abundant, even during the summer. Stream sources or wells may be used. However, water temperature, power and pumps, and protection from pollution, parasites, disease organisms, and undesirable wild fish should be considered.

After land purchase the largest cost is pond construction, ranging from $500 to $5,000 and more for earth moving, draining, and grass cover. Cost of installing the water system depends on whether stream or well water is to be used, and on whether an oxygen-adding method is installed. The largest operating expenses are finger lings and feed. Other expenses are chemicals for control of disease, parasites, weeds, and cost of maintaining ponds. During the first year there is no return on the capital investment.

The most serious risks can be divided as follows: Variation in water quality, disease and parasitism, poor quality fingerlings, and vandalism and theft. Production risk and risk associated with marketing can be controlled through good management. Price risk may occur, however, as consumers' tastes change; as competitors move into and saturate a market; or as other meat substitutes become significantly cheaper.

There are many small businesses in america. Small businesses can have as few as one worker (the owner) or as many as four workers. A small business is self-employed. Often a whole family works together in a small business.

Three main things are necessary in planning a fish farming business. First, are your personal qualities right for the business. Second, have you thought about what you would raise and who your customers might be. Finally have you learned about the legal requirements for running a fish farm. It is very important that you have what it takes to run a fish farming business. You need business skills to keep the fish farm making money. You must like working on a fish farm and should be able to work without a lot of people around. You must want to be your own boss. You will need to work very hard to make the business succeed. You will have to be good at solving problems because you will be in charge.

If you decide to start your business as a sole proprietorship this means that you would get to keep all of the profits of the fish farming business. However, you would also be responsible for all of the debts if the business fails. There are other legal forms of business, and it is important to know what would be best for your business.

Fish farming owners can't start their farms just anywhere. They have to think about several things in considering a location. Is it too close to town? Is there enough land for your needs? Is there enough water for your needs? Are the right buildings and equipment there, or can you put them in pretty easily? Will it be easy to sell other products

Fish Farming

Aquaculture, possibly the oldest form of agriculture, is on the increase. Channel catfish and other catfish, trout, abalone, and oysters are among the products of these special farming industries.

Fish farming can be profitable, but it is far from a get-rich quick venture. Success depends on excellent business management, together with plenty of technical know-how and the ability to keep up with changing technology. Risk is moderate to high. Experts emphasize the desirability of visiting successful farms before investing.

The profitability of catfish farming is greatly influenced by available marketing alternatives, and selecting markets is an important part of fish farm management.

Many catfish farmers sell directly to wholesale processing plants, especially in the states of Mississippi and Alabama. Nationally, about 27 percent of the catfish production goes to this outlet. Some processors enter into lower contractual agreements with growers.

More than 40 percent of commercially grown catfish goes to recreational markets. Growers often set aside fee-fishing ponds on their farms and stock them heavily for public recreational fishing. They either collect a flat fee for fishing or charge the fisher for what he/she catches. This marketing method usually brings the farmer top dollar for the product. Some farmers choose to sell live or dressed fish to local buyers at the fish farm. About 31 percent of all fish sold are marketed in this manner, and some farmers find this method highly profitable.

A few fish farmers operate restaurants in which they serve some or all of the fish they produce. This can be very profitable if proper restaurant management is exercised. For channel catfish farming, a recommended size farm is 60 land acres: 40 acres farmed intensively in ponds of 5 to 10 acres each, the rest in roads, dams, storage, and so on. Soil borings should be analyzed to make sure ponds will not require the added expense of linings to make them hold water. Ponds must be completely protected from any flood runoff, and the site must be protected legally from aerial crop spraying on adjacent land. In addition, there must be no toxic chemical residue from nearby recent operations. Drainage from the farm into existing streams is legally prohibited in some areas.

Using the newspaper is a good way to get workers. But not everyone who answers the ad will be a good worker. You should also ask each person about her or his training and experience. Then you can talk to the most qualified ones in person. When you talk to people about the job, you should learn as much as possible about their work. Workers need to know as much as possible about the job. That way, they can decide if it's right for them or not.

Five steps you can use to choose a person to work for you are: 1. Writing a job description; 2. Advertising the job to people who might want to take it; 3. Looking at the training and experience of the people who applied; 4. Talking to applicants about their work and about what the job would be like; 5. Checking references from employers. After you have hired your employee, you should help her or him learn about the job. You may need to do some extra training if the person hasn't done all the jobs you want to have done.

In any business you will need supplies. In a fish farming business you have to keep careful track of the supplies you buy and use. This is because all your supplies and other costs have to be reported to the government at tax time. You also have to keep track of supplies so that you don't run out of anything. This is especially true when your farm is growing. If you don't watch how your supply needs are changing, you may get caught short at a bad time. There are three things to think about in choosing where to buy supplies: 1. The merchandise -does the supplier carry everything you need? Can you get the brands and amounts you need? 2. The services—can you get quick, reliable delivery? If you have problems or complaints, will the supplier handle them fairly? 3. The prices— are the prices reasonable? Can you arrange to buy on credit? It may be a good idea to buy from two suppliers, or from even more.

Profit is the amount left over after the operating expenses are paid. Profit is spent to pay taxes and expand the business. Profit is also used for the fish farmers to live on. They buy their food, clothes, and furniture out of the profit. The money brought in from the sale of your fish farming products, called income, must be enough to pay the operating expenses and provide some profit. If it doesn't, after a while the farm will go out of business.

Customer demand or desire to buy can be different for different fish products. One year freshwater catfish may be popular; the next year fry/fingerling may be more popular; and the next yera brood fish. There are fashions in fish just as in clothes. In setting prices, you have to be aware of customer demand. You also have to be aware of the prices your competitors are charging for the same products. The best way for you to check other prices is to visit your competitors now and then to compare prices. You

from there? You won't want to choose a location that is very close to a city. The closer you get to a town, the more the land costs. This is because close-in land may be good for houses. People will pay more for houses than for open land—a lot more. Builders know that, so they are willing to pay a lot for land, too. Fish farmers are likely to find that such land costs far too much for them to afford. If they are paying more for land than the income they can bring in, they won't stay in business long.

Also, if a farm is in an area of houses, other problems may come up. People may complain about the noise or smells of a fish farm. Certain areas will have zoning restrictions preventing fish farms from locating there anyway.

Starting any small business takes money. Usually you need a loan from a bank or a government agency. To get a loan, you need to give the loan officer three kinds of information in writing: Personal information on yourself; a description of your business; and a statement of your starting expenses, called a statement of financial need. Personal information is often written in the form of a resume'. A resume' shows your education and experience and gives names of references.

A business description should tell the loan officer everything important about the business. A fish farming business description has the following parts: Kind of business and products sold; market; and plans for success.

The statement of financial need has three parts: Starting expenses; money on hand; and loan needed. A bank will want you to raise your own money as well as use its loan to start your business. It may take several years of saving to get enough money. Sometimes your family can lend you money. The loan needed equals the starting expenses minus the money on hand. It is important to think carefully about how much money you need. If you ask for too much, you may not get the loan. If you ask for too little, your business may go broke.

Most small businesses hire extra workers at some time. To get good work done, you have to decide exactly what your worker should do. Then you have to find a good worker. A good worker knows how to do the job and also is reliable. Another important part of good work is how well people get along together. Both owners and employees need to think about this.

The way you divide the work is important because it determines the kind of worker you should hire. Each way of dividing the work means a different set of skills needed by your worker. That means different kinds of training and experience needed. To be sure of what kind of worker you need, it helps to write down a job description for each worker. A job description should list all the kinds of things the worker will do. As the owner, you should have a description, too. That way, everybody knows who does what.

Notes _____

might also check the newspapers to see the prices listed. You have to know how much fish products you are selling and how much money is coming in and going out. This is how you know if your business is making or losing money. You have to report income and expenses to the government to pay taxes. Good records also help you decide if you should expand your business or cut it back. You need to keep records of the fish farm's expenses. Keep copies of all of the bills and sales slips you receive when you buy supplies. Keeping a record for each kind of expense is simpler than keeping one record for everything.

A fish farm owner can never stop trying to improve his or her business. Customer demand for fish products may change, and prices may change. You have to keep careful track of changes like these. You have to know exactly how your business is doing so you can make changes to keep up to date.

A profit and loss statement shows total income and total expenses over a period of time, usually a year. Net profit is the difference between total revenue and total expenses in a year. Net profit is used to pay the owner's salaries and taxes and to make improvements on the farm. An easy way to see the whole picture of a business is to figure the profit ratio and the expense ratio for each year. The profit ratio for any year is the net profit divided by the revenues. The expense ratio is the expenses divided by the revenues. To increase net profits, a business must do one of two things: Reduce expenses; or increase revenues. Reducing expenses can be done by looking for suppliers who sell cheaper supplies. Increasing revenues can be done by raising your fish price or increasing your fish production.

INSURANCE CHECKLIST

TYPE OF INSURANCE	PURCHASE	DO NOT PURCHASE
PROPERTY INSURANCE:		
Fire	_____	_____
Windstorm	_____	_____
Hail	_____	_____
Smoke	_____	_____
Explosion	_____	_____
Vandalism	_____	_____
Water Damage	_____	_____
Glass	_____	_____
LIABILITY INSURANCE	_____	_____
WORKERS' COMPENSATION	_____	_____
BUSINESS INTERRUPTION	_____	_____
DISHONESTY:		
Fidelity	_____	_____
Robbery	_____	_____
Burglary	_____	_____
Comprehensive	_____	_____
PERSONAL:		
Health	_____	_____
Life	_____	_____
Key Personnel	_____	_____

Appendix D

Business Web Site
an
Effective Marketing Tool

More than 100 million people use the Internet each day. A website offers help in marketing your small business. Your web site can help level the playing field for small businesses who compete with big businesses. It can enable small business to expand their business nationally or internationally.

What makes a good web site?

A good web site shows by doing; it proves rather than states. Instead of making claims, it provides evidence.

Evidence can take several forms:

- Case Studies showing how your efforts solved a previous client's problems.

- Testimonials from satisfied clients.

- Reprints of articles you've written or reviews of your work.

Education, however, remains the best way to establish credibility. To the extent prospects leave your web site better informed about your product or service, the easier it is to gain their respect (and their purchase order).

Three steps to creating your own business web site.

Today's tools make web publishing accessible to small businesses without programming experience. For example, Microsoft® Publisher 97 includes PageWizard design assistants, web deign elements and design checkers to help your build a workable web site.

Step one:

Choose a structure and a look. Your site should be structured and designed to best tell your story. But where do you start? Using the Page Wizard, you can choose from pre-designed options that can later be customized so that establishing a structure and "look" is easy.

Step two:

Tell your story. Next, simply select the sample headlines and text provided and replace them with words that describe what you have to offer.

Step three:

Check your work and post your site. The design in Publisher 97 goes through your web site element by element, identifying potential problems. Then, the web publishing wizard guides you through the process of posting your web site on the local Internet service provider or on-line service of your choice.

Remember, with millions of web sites, you may have to market your web site as well as your small business to get traffic for your business. The web site can be an inexpensive way of effectively building your small business.

10 tips for Web Site Online Marketing

1. Put up a simple web page.
2. Use a name that will attract people
3. Give away advice and information
4. Have lots of e-mail correspondence
5. Provide customized pages for users.
6. Visit user groups
7. Get on mailing lists
8. Arrange links with related sites
9. Make sure you're in every possible directory
10. Do not "SPAM"

Special Appendix

Web Site Marketing

INDEX

Business Books

Telephone 1-616-275-7287 • 1-517-684-1184 • Fax 1-517-684-3072

How to Start and Manage:

ISBN 1-57916-000-X	An Apparel Store Business
ISBN 1-57916-001-8	A Word Processing Service Business
ISBN 1-57916-002-6	A Garden Center Business
ISBN 1-57916-003-4	A Hair Styling Shop Business
ISBN 1-57916-004-2	A Bicycle Shop Business
ISBN 1-57916-005-0	A Travel Agency Business
ISBN 1-57916-006-9	An Answering Service Business
ISBN 1-57916-007-7	A Health Spa Business
ISBN 1-57916-008-5	A Restaurant Business
ISBN 1-57916-009-3	A Specialty Food Store Business
ISBN 1-57916-010-7	A Welding Business
ISBN 1-57916-011-5	A Day Care Center Business
ISBN 1-57916-012-3	A Flower and Plant Store Business
ISBN 1-57916-013-1	A Construction Electrician Business
ISBN 1-57916-014-X	A Housecleaning Service Business
ISBN 1-57916-015-8	A Nursing Service Business
ISBN 1-57916-016-6	A Bookkeeping Service Business
ISBN 1-57916-017-4	A Secretarial Service Business
ISBN 1-57916-018-2	A Bed and Breakfast Business
ISBN 1-57916-019-0	An Energy Specialist Business
ISBN 1-57916-020-4	A Guard Service Business
ISBN 1-57916-021-2	A Software Design Business
ISBN 1-57916-022-0	An Air Conditioning & Heating Business
ISBN 1-57916-023-9	A Plumbing Service Business
ISBN 1-57916-024-7	A Sewing Service Business
ISBN 1-57916-025-5	A Carpentry Service Business
ISBN 1-57916-026-3	A Home Attendant Service Business
ISBN 1-57916-027-1	A Tree Service Business
ISBN 1-57916-028-X	A Dairy Farming Business
ISBN 1-57916-029-8	A Farm Equipment Repair Service Business
ISBN 1-57916-030-1	A Children's Clothing Store Business
ISBN 1-57916-031-X	A Women's Apparel Store
ISBN 1-57916-032-8	A Convenience Food Store Business
ISBN 1-57916-033-6	A Pest Control Service Business
ISBN 1-57916-034-4	A Printing Business
ISBN 1-57916-035-2	An Ice Cream Business
ISBN 1-57916-036-0	A Mail Order Business
ISBN 1-57916-037-9	A Bookstore Business
ISBN 1-57916-038-7	A Home Furnishing Business
ISBN 1-57916-039-5	A Retail Florist Business
ISBN 1-57916-040-9	A Radio-Television Repair Shop Business
ISBN 1-57916-041-7	A Dry Cleaning Business
ISBN 1-57916-042-5	A Hardware Store Business
ISBN 1-57916-043-3	A Marine Retailing Business
ISBN 1-57916-044-1	An Office Products Business
ISBN 1-57916-045-X	A Pharmacy Business
ISBN 1-57916-046-8	A Fish Farming Business
ISBN 1-57916-047-6	A Personal Referral Service Business
ISBN 1-57916-048-4	A Solar Energy Business
ISBN 1-57916-049-2	A Building Service Contracting Business
ISBN 1-57916-050-6	A Retail Decorating Products Business
ISBN 1-57916-051-4	A Sporting Goods Store Business
ISBN 1-57916-052-2	A Retail Grocery Store
ISBN 1-57916-053-0	A Cosmetology Business
ISBN 1-57916-054-9	A Franchised Business
ISBN 1-57916-055-7	An Electronics Industry Consulting Practice Business
ISBN 1-57916-056-5	An Independent Consulting Practice Business
ISBN 1-57916-057-3	An Independent Trucking Business
ISBN 1-57916-058-1	An Accounting Service Business

ISBN 1-57916-059-X	A Nursery Business
ISBN 1-57916-060-3	A Seminar Promotion Business
ISBN 1-57916-061-1	A Bar & Cocktail Lounge Business
ISBN 1-57916-062-X	A Wheelchair Transportation Business
ISBN 1-57916-063-8	A Fertilizer and Pesticide Business
ISBN 1-57916-064-6	A Desktop Publishing Business
ISBN 1-57916-065-4	A Crime Prevention Business
ISBN 1-57916-066-2	A Gift Shop Business
ISBN 1-57916-067-0	A Handcraft Success Business
ISBN 1-57916-068-9	A Coin-Operated Laundries Business
ISBN 1-57916-069-7	A Property Management Business
ISBN 1-57916-070-0	An Auto Supply Store Business
ISBN 1-57916-071-9	A Men's Apparel Store Business
ISBN 1-57916-072-7	A Temporary Help Service Business
ISBN 1-57916-073-5	An Advertising Agency Business
ISBN 1-57916-074-3	A Firewood Sales Business
ISBN 1-57916-075-1	A Children's Bookstore Business
ISBN 1-57916-076-X	A Used Bookstore Business
ISBN 1-57916-077-8	A Sandwich Shop Deli Business
ISBN 1-57916-078-6	An Instant Print/Copy Shop
ISBN 1-57916-079-4	A Gift Specialty Store Business
ISBN 1-57916-080-8	A Gift Basket Service Business
ISBN 1-57916-081-6	A Hospitality Management Business
ISBN 1-57916-082-4	A Hotel Business
ISBN 1-57916-083-2	A Catering Service Business
ISBN 1-57916-084-0	A Carpet-Cleaning Service Business
ISBN 1-57916-085-9	A Window-Washing Service Business
ISBN 1-57916-086-7	An Innkeeping Service Business
ISBN 1-57916-087-5	An Apartment Preparation Service
ISBN 1-57916-088-3	A Kiosks and Cart Business
ISBN 1-57916-089-1	A Janitorial Service Business
ISBN 1-57916-090-5	A Medical Claims Processing Business
ISBN 1-57916-091-3	A Nursing Home Care Business
ISBN 1-57916-092-1	A Home Health Care Business
ISBN 1-57916-093-X	A Referral Services Business
ISBN 1-57916-094-8	A Hair Styling Salon Business
ISBN 1-57916-095-6	A Child Care Service Business

How-To Business Books

ISBN 1-57916-096-4	How to Buy and Sell A Business
ISBN 1-57916-097-2	How to Advertise A Small Business
ISBN 1-57916-098-0	How to Write A Successful Business Plan
ISBN 1-57916-099-9	How to Finance Your Business for the 21st Century
ISBN 1-57916-100-6	How to Market Your Business for the 21st Century

To Order Business Plans

Please Remit To:

Lewis & Renn Associates
10315 Harmony Drive
Interlochen, Michigan 49643

Business Book # 1-57916-_____ Title _____

Business Book # 1-57916-_____ Title _____

Name _____

Address _____

City _____

State _____ Zip _____

Business Book _____

U.S. Shipping & Postage __$ 3.00__

Total _____

Library Discount - 20%
Retail Discount - 20%
$3.00 Postage & Handling
$18.95 Each

Step-by-Step Guides To Start, Manage & Market Your Own Business

4th Printing!

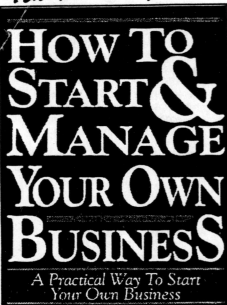

New!

3rd Printing!

How To Start & Manage Your Own Business

For anyone who is looking to start-up a new business, this *step-by-step guide* includes planning, managing, marketing and promotion. **$18.95**

Soft Cover • 104 Pages
5 1/2" x 8 1/2" 0-9628759-0-2 ©1992

How to Start & Manage a Home Based Business

This book provides the knowledge and tools necessary to successfully plan, design, and start up a new business in a practical way. With a step-by-step guide for planning, managing, marketing and promotion of a small business, in an easy-to-read and easy-to-understand format. The guidelines presented will help you pursue dreams of independence and financial success. **$18.95**

Soft Cover • 135 Pages
5 1/2" x 8 1/2" 1-887005-11-0 © 1996

How To Start A Participative Management Program

A concise guide for small to midsi[ze] companies that is easy to read and foll[ow] *Step-by-step planning, managing a[nd] marketing of a small business* • H[ow] to empower and involve employee[s] Contains tools for measuring employ[ee] work environment. **$18.9[5]**

Soft Cover • 93 Pages •
5 1/2" x 8 1/2", 0-9628759 ©1992

ABOUT THE AUTHORS

Jerre G. Lewis and Leslie D. Renn are both experienced professionals concerning small business management and entrepreneurship. For more than twenty years Mr. Lewis has been involved with business education at college level and the development of a series of small business seminars. He is a Certified Education Specialist for the U.S. Small Business Administration Volunteer Counseling Program. Mr. Renn is a business owner, entrepreneur, a small business consultant, and like Mr. Lewis. is involved with college level management instruction & business seminars. He also has extensive experience in large industry administration. Mr. Lewis and Mr. Renn received bachelors and masters degrees from Michigan universities, and both work and live in northern Michigan.